HOPE
FOR THE WORLD

A Christian Looks At World Religions

Hinduism - Judaism - Buddhism
Confucianism - Christianity - Islam

Carl Mays

The Lincoln-Bradley Publishing Group
NY
Produced in conjunction with
Creative Living, Inc.
Gatlinburg, TN
USA

The Lincoln-Bradley Publishing Group
c/o Creative Living, Inc.
P.O. Box 808
Gatlinburg, TN 37738
(865) 436-4150
Email: Hope@carlmays.com

———————

Publisher's Cataloging-in-Publication

Mays, Carl
    Hope for the world: a Christian looks at world reli-
gions: Hinduism, Judaism, Buddhism, Confucianism,
Christianity, Islam / Carl Mays.
    p. cm.
    ISBN: 1-879111-01-2

    1. Religions -- doctrines, quotations, maxims, etc.
    2. Conduct of life -- quotations, maxims, etc.
    3. Values -- quotations, maxims, etc.
    4. Success -- quotations, maxims, etc. I. Title

BL80.2.M39   2001   291
                          QBI01-201283

Book & Cover Design/Make-up by Mary Schultz
Crescent Color Printing - Gatlinburg, TN

Printed on approved acid-free paper

1 2 3 4 5 6 7 8 9 10

Contents

Prayer For Our
Global Community

Lord ...

Make me an instrument of your peace;
Where there is hatred, let me sow love;
Where there is injury, pardon;
Where there is discord, union;
Where there is doubt, faith;
Where there is despair, hope;
Where there is darkness, light;
And where there is sadness, joy ...

*- Francis of Assisi
(1182-1226)*

The Purpose Of This Book

On September 11, 2001, someone asked me, "What do Muslims believe and how can Christians relate to them?" This book is in response to that question. But it goes way beyond that question.

When terrorists slammed jetliners into the World Trade Center and the Pentagon, and crashed in rural Pennsylvania, people were shocked, grieved and outraged. There were great heroic efforts and an outpouring of love and prayer. There were also many questions, and the chasm that separates world religions was widened. Since the immediate suspects were Arab Muslims, there was especially a swift outcry and reaction against the Islamic faith.

In any comparative religion course, students quickly learn that the history of religion is not always pretty. Sometimes it is downright ugly. Throughout history, there have been atrocious acts committed in the name of religion, including Christianity. Yet, Christians realize that religion practiced in its purest form is what gives life meaning. It is what carries us through challenging and devastating times, drawing us closer to God and to one another.

With other Christians, I find comfort in John

3:16, "For God so loved the world that He gave His only begotten Son, that whoever believes in Him should not perish but have everlasting life." Believing that Christ died as a sacrifice for everyone brings us hope in any situation.

With other Christians, I take to heart the great commission issued by Christ in Matthew 28:19, "Go therefore and make disciples of all the nations, baptizing them in the name of the Father and of the Son and of the Holy Spirit."

As we feel compelled to share the Gospel of Christ, we must also feel compelled to respect and love people of other religious faiths. This is where our relating to them begins - accepting all humans as precious creations, created in God's image. All real missionary and evangelistic work begins with this premise. The work begins with a loving concern for the physical, mental and spiritual condition of every person, worldwide.

As Christians, we must remind ourselves that many people of other religions are trying to *do the right thing*. In response to the question, "What do Muslims believe and how can Christians relate to them?", this book presents a synopsis of Islam. It also presents synopses of the other five major religions of the world. As you will discover, each religion is easier to understand when we see how it relates to other religions.

These synopses include evidence that none of these religions was founded with the intention of promoting unkindness, improprieties, hate or acts of terrorism. Following the terrorist attacks on America, Aly Abuzaakouk, executive director of the American Muslim Council, said, "There is no faith on earth that can condone this heinous crime." President George W. Bush referred to the terrorists as attackers of the Islamic faith.

President Bush and other leaders have encouraged us to inspect the religious beliefs of people before assaulting them verbally or physically, as individuals or as a group. Hopefully, this book will help readers to better understand some basic religious beliefs and to improve dialogue with people of other faiths. Not only is this important now, but it will continue to grow in importance as our global community becomes more like a familiar neighborhood.

In no way does this small book attempt to delve into all the methods devised by humans to seek spiritual fulfillment and meaning in this life and in the hereafter. Today, there are approximately six billion people inhabiting earth and it is estimated that well over four billion profess religious beliefs. Therefore, it behooves everyone to be somewhat knowledgeable of the faiths that people claim as their own.

As a professional speaker and consultant in the areas of leadership and human relations, I have had an opportunity to work with over 2500 groups nationally and internationally. My clients have been corporations, associations, religious institutions, sports teams, schools and universities. As I have prepared for programs through the years, I have done research to discover what I have in common with my clients.

After determining the common ground that I share with my clients, then I conduct a needs analysis and determine what I can do to help my clients meet their needs. This is the approach I believe we should use in relating to people of other faiths. What beliefs do we have in common? What are the apparent needs?

The majority of participants in my sessions have been professing Christians. Next in number would be people of the Jewish faith, then Muslims. Hinduism, Buddhism and Confucianism have also been represented. In the last few years, my audiences have been more diverse than ever before.

These six religions have larger followings, have been in existence longer, have made greater historical impact and continue to have greater influence today. Christianity, Judaism and Islam are generally referred to as monotheistic (one God), while Hinduism, Buddhism and Confucianism are generally referred to as polytheistic (multiple gods). Some scholars do not consider Confucianism to be a religion, but you will see more on that when you come to the synopses.

After presenting a synopsis of each of the religions, the larger portion of this book will be dedicated to sharing the principles the six religions have in common. There are, of course, some major differences among the faiths. You will see, however, how all six share some common principles. When these parallel principles are actually adhered to by their proponents, relationships between people, within families and among nations can be strengthened.

From Seed To Fruit

The seed for this book was planted a number of years ago when I was a graduate student working toward my degree in religious education. One of my research projects dealt with the history and beliefs of the world's major religions. I became extremely intrigued by the founding and development of these faiths. As I compared their scriptures and other written materials, the differences were clear but the common principles were evident.

The seed was nourished in the 1990s when I developed and taught a class titled *World Religions - Distilled*. The seed began to sprout on September 11, 2001, when the question regarding Muslims was asked.

As a Christian, I believe that by faith in the life, death and resurrection of Christ a person becomes a child of God for eternity, and that by good works this faith is evidenced in a person's daily life. At the same time, I know that other religions offer constructive lifestyles to their proponents. As you will see in this book, other religions have some solid guidelines that promote good works.

As a Christian, I accept the words of Jesus in John 14:6, "I am the way, the truth, and the life. No one comes to the Father except through Me." Yet, at the same time, other Christians and I must realize that we are not the only people in the world who advocate high moral and ethical values. And, there are many professing Christians whose moral and ethical values never reach the lofty heights of some people of other faiths.

I have had the privilege of interacting with people in various religious venues, which includes teaching an adult Bible class for 24 years and working with the Fellowship of Christian Athletes for 21 years. It also includes planning and leading in dozens of conferences for several different denominations and writing for several Christian and secular publishers.

I had the opportunity to serve as president of Religious Heritage of America, a national organization that promotes the values upon which America was founded. This afforded me the privilege of working extensively with people of Judeo-Christian influence and to have dialogue with people of other religions.

Earlier in my career, I was a city wide youth director in three different areas of the country and was a teacher and coach. While acquiring my graduate degree, I counseled at a home for unwed mothers, at a charity hospital and at an international marine hospital. This service allowed me to experience how people of various faiths deal with challenges and pain and everyday life.

My studies and experiences have revealed to me how people have always searched for hope and guidance in their lives. People have always been drawn to a power superior to humankind. That is why there has never been a civilization in recorded history that has not worshipped God or gods.

In Romans 1:19-20, the apostle Paul wrote, ". . . what may be known of God is manifest in them, for God has shown it to them. For since the creation of the world His invisible attributes are clearly seen . . . " In this, Paul emphasizes that everyone is born with an inner knowledge of God. That is why the search for God continues and will always continue until the end of time. That is why it is vital for us to relate to others in the search.

We are imperfect people living in an imperfect

world. We are a part of one another, affecting and influencing one another. This reemphasizes the importance of our knowing people and their religions, relating to them appropriately and sharing with them in a caring, loving manner.

This also reemphasizes the importance of understanding the parallel principles we share with one another. As we talk with people about eternity, we also need to encourage them - and ourselves - to actually live by the day-to-day guidelines that are common in our religions.

Where Do We Begin?

On earth, people will never agree upon matters of religion and how best to seek spiritual fulfillment and meaning. To the contrary, even denominations, components, streams or tributaries within each faith will never agree upon certain issues. However, when more people live by the personal and human relations principles that *are* agreed upon by the major religions of the world, our global community will be changed in a very positive way.

When more people apply the fundamental goodness upon which our religions are based, every nation will be enhanced tremendously. When more people strive to practice the basic parallel principles of the six major world religions, without distortion, rationalization and manipulation, then we will discover that unkindness, improprieties, heinous crimes and acts of terrorism will not so completely saturate our world.

In the pages that follow, the parallel principles are presented in a simple, distilled manner that just about any proponent of any religion can understand. The real challenge for people of all religions, however, is to have the courage to apply these spiritual agreements to our daily lives, not just to understand them.

Where do we begin? We can begin by gaining a better understanding of who we are and how we fit into the total world composite.

According to research, if our world were a community of 100 people, it would consist of approximately:

* 58 Asians
* 12 Africans
* 10 East & West Europeans
* 8 Latin Americans
* 6 (Former) Soviets (Geographically)
* 5 North Americans
* 1 Australian & New Zealander

The language spoken by these 100 people of our global community would consist of approximately:

* 17 Mandarin
* 9 English
* 8 Hindi/Urdu
* 6 Spanish
* 6 Russian
* 4 Arabic
* 50 assorted languages of over 200, including, in order of usage, Bengali, Portuguese, Indonesian, Japanese, German and French.

The religions claimed by these 100 people of our global community would consist of approximately:

* 33 Professed Christians
* 18 Professed Muslims (Islam)
* 17 with no professed beliefs
* 13 Professed Hindus
* 6 Professed Buddhists
* 4 Professed Atheists
* 1 Professed Jew
* 8 all other professed religions combined

Drawing from this information, here are brief synopses of the major religions from which the book's parallel principles are taken. They are listed in the order in which it is commonly believed they came into existence.

HINDUISM. Said to be the oldest of the current major religions, Hinduism was brought to India approximately 3,500-4,000 years ago by

Aryans from Eastern Europe, and most of the Hindus live in India today. The religion has no single identifiable founder, and is a complex religion with many sects. Its overall theology cannot be succinctly stated due to the many tributaries and changes over the years.

Hinduism, however, as a religion and a way of life, teaches that the universe undergoes endless cycles of creation, disintegration and preservation. It emphasizes that all souls are constantly evolving and progressing toward union with God, and that all intellect, creativity and imagination are derived from God, who is the supreme Knowledge, pure Intelligence and Consciousness.

In Hinduism, *Karma* (fate) is the moral and physical law of cause and effect by which each individual creates his or her own future destiny by accepting personal responsibility and accountability for thoughts, words and deeds.

During the middle of the 20th century, Mohandas Gandhi epitomized the essence of Hinduism. While leaders such as Hitler and Stalin destroyed both peace and people, Gandhi led the British withdrawal from India in a nonviolent manner. While destructive leaders belittled people, Gandhi took India's "untouchables" and renamed them "God's people," helping to raise them to human stature.

Inspired by Gandhi, Martin Luther King, Jr., a Christian minister, emulated his nonviolent strategy to lead the civil rights movement in America.

Hinduism realizes that people seek pleasure, success and fulfillment, but emphasizes that true fulfillment is not centered on personal preoccupation. It stresses that's one's growth moves beyond limited, individual indulgences and focuses upon a duty to others while moving closer to God.

Thus, it is no surprise that Gandhi, well-educated and at one time rather well-off materially, was worth less than two dollars in worldly possessions when he died. Sacrificing his own life in order to bring attention to his cause and to the plight of his people, he weighed less than 100 pounds at his death.

It is believed the religion's name came into existence when in the Valley of the Indus the group who had earlier crossed the *Hindu Kush Mountains* began a verbal tradition of the earliest known scriptures, the *Vedas*.

Later, when the scriptures were recorded, they were divided into the four *Vedas: Rig, Yajur, Sama* and *Atharva*. The *Upanishads* later became portions of the *Vedas*. Additional scriptures and supplements to the scriptures followed.

Although some other religions might not agree,

Hinduism emphasizes that the major religions offer various paths to God and that no one religion has a monopoly on salvation. From the start, the Vedas announced Hinduism's contention that the various religions are but different languages through which God speaks to the human heart.

Ramakrishna, considered the greatest Hindu saint of the 19th century, wrote: "God has made different religions to suit different aspirations, times and countries. All doctrines are only so many paths; but a path is by no means God Himself. Indeed, one can reach God if one follows any of the paths with whole-hearted devotion. One may eat a cake with icing either straight or sidewise. It will taste sweet either way."

Though other religions may not accept the Hindu belief of all paths leading to God, the belief does promote "peace on earth" among all people, even if it does not reach agreement with other religions about where all people might spend eternity.

JUDAISM. As documented in the *Old Testament* of the *Bible* and accompanying Jewish literature, Judaism as we know it today was born around 4,000 years ago in the Middle East among the ancient Jews, a nomadic people. They wandered from place to place in the Arabian desert, constantly seeking better pastures for their sheep and goats. They were tribal, divided into clans, originally worshiping many gods - of water, trees, fire, storms, mountains . . .

But Abraham, one of the greatest of all the early Jewish patriarchs, learned to place one God, *Yahweh*, above all others. Abraham declared that the strength of *Yahweh* was far greater than the combined strength of all the other gods. Because of Abraham's faith, God made a pact with him to accept the Jews as God's chosen people and to bless them so long as they acknowledged him alone as their God and responded to his leadership. In turn, God expected the Jews eventually to become a blessing to the entire world.

After God led Abraham to "step out on faith," the Jews left Ur of the Chaldees, an ancient city in Lower Mesopotamia, for the purpose of establishing a nation. Crossing the Euphrates River in their migration, they picked up the name "Hebrews" from a word which means "to cross over."

To Abraham and his wife Sarah was born Isaac. Jacob and his twin brother Esau descended from Isaac and his wife Rebecca. Jacob later was renamed Israel by God, and Israel was the father of twelve sons who became heads of the twelve tribes of the Israel nation.

One of Jacob's sons was Joseph, who was sold into slavery by his jealous brothers and carried into

Egypt. Joseph rose to a position of leadership under the powerful Pharaoh and brought his family and his people to live in the abundant land of Egypt. Eventually, however, another Pharaoh came into power and enslaved the Hebrews.

Because the Hebrews were increasing in number, the Pharaoh ordered all the male babies killed. But Moses, grandson of Levi, a son of Jacob, was adopted by Pharaoh's daughter when she found him hidden in the bulrushes. Unknowingly, Pharaoh's daughter engaged Moses' own mother to care for the child.

When in his 80's, Moses was called by God to unify the Jews, to develop a creed of right living, to unite the tribes with a bond of common worship and the promise of deliverance from the Egyptian captivity. Moses emphasized Hebrew liberty in the name of a righteous God, who became not only paramount among deities, but "the only true and living God."

Moses led the Hebrews out of bondage, then held them together during 40 years of wandering in the wilderness. Before entering the "promised land" of Canaan under the leadership of Joshua, these people had been induced by Moses to worship only God (*Yahweh*, also referred to as *Jehovah*), thus paving the way for the monotheism which is the basis of Western theology.

The *Torah*, containing God's instruction and direction for Israel, teaches that all humanity is created in the image of God, and that God speaks to all human beings in various ways. The ultimate goal of humans is to affirm the Sovereignty of God and to establish harmony and peace - *Shalom* - among all people. The *Talmud*, which constitutes the Jewish civil and religious law, serves as a written means to this end.

Looking upon our global community as the "community" referred to in Judaism's *TA'ANIT*, we can see its relevance to the subject matter of this entire book: *"If the community is in trouble, one must not say, 'I will go to my house, and eat and drink, and peace shall be with thee, O my soul.' But the person must share in the trouble of the community, even as Moses did. One who shares in its troubles is worthy to see its consolation."*

BUDDHISM. Around 560 B.C. (or B.C.E. - Before the Common Era - as Jews prefer to render the period), Siddhartha Gautama of the Sakhya clan was born in Northeast India. It is claimed that his father was a king, and at age sixteen Gautama married a neighboring princess, Yasodhara.

Gautama appeared to "have it all." However, he grew discontent and unfulfilled in his twenties, which led to a complete break with the life he knew. Forsaking all, he began to search for meaning in life, beginning by going into the wilderness to seek enlightenment. Eventually, he sought out the foremost Hindu masters of the day. Through them he began a spiritual pilgrimage, from which he emerged the *Buddha*.

Buddha's name developed as a result of his answer to questions pertaining to whom and what he was. He responded to the questions by saying he was not a god, not an angel, not a saint. He said, "I am awake." The Sanskrit (classical literary language of ancient India) root word *"budh"* denotes both "to awaken" and "to know." *Buddha*, then, means the "Enlightened One" or the "Awakened One."

As gleaned from Buddhist principles presented in this book, the reader will understand why Buddha was considered a very wise person, able to creativity face and solve problems of all sorts. At the same time, he emphasized a religion of compassion and concern.

A thread that runs through the teachings of Buddha is the emphasis on the realm of life in which there is neither age nor death. Because life on earth is subject to disease, to the wear and tear of old age and eventually death, Buddha, like Hindu's Gandhi, dismissed the importance of personal fleshly pleasures. Therefore, it is easy to understand why he often denounced the sins of envy, jealously and covetousness.

Interestingly, just as Christianity grew out of Judaism and built upon it, so Buddhism grew out of Hinduism and built upon it. Just as Jesus of Nazareth later viewed his own Judaism as a religion that was not being practiced as it should, and being corrupted by religious leaders, so Buddha viewed Hinduism and Hindu leaders of his time.

It is commonly agreed that if a religion is to have an opportunity to fulfill its intended purposes, six areas of concern have to be dealt with and managed properly. These areas are authority, rituals, speculation, tradition, grace and mysteries.

Authority can be abused; rituals can become mechanical and empty; speculation can lead to the "swallowing of a camel while choking on a gnat;" tradition can become dead weight as people believe or do something because "it's always been done that way;" God's grace can be taken for granted, with people believing God will take care of them even when the people ignore God's will and leadership; and the true spiritual mysteries can lead to perverse obsession with the occult and miracles for the sake of miracles.

Buddha found these areas of Hinduism in dire need of "getting back to the basics," and much of his work was spent in trying to purify, clarify and build upon what he had learned earlier from the Hindu masters he respected.

Buddha traveled and taught in the Ganges River basin until his death at 84. From the basin area, Buddhism spread through much of India. But, by the end of the 13th century, as a result of several hundred years of foreign invasions, the religion disappeared from its land of origin.

By the time it disappeared from India, however, it had already spread to Southeast Asia, becoming the dominant religion in such places as Vietnam, Cambodia, Thailand, Burma and Laos. It also reached Central and East Asia, becoming dominant in Japan, China, Korea, Mongolia and Tibet. It continued to extend throughout various Himalayan areas, and made its way to North America.

CONFUCIANISM. Because of its lack of emphasis on theology, which is the study of God or gods, some scholars do not even consider Confucianism a religion. They say it is purely an emphasis on a moral and ethical lifestyle. Kung Fu-tzu is reverently spoken of by the Chinese as the *First Teacher,* because he stands first in rank, known as *Confucius.*

Confucius was born around 550 B.C. and died in 479 B.C. Not much is known about his home life, but it is documented that he came from a modest family. He wrote, "When young, I was without rank and in humble circumstances." His father died before he was three, leaving his upbringing to a materially poor but very loving mother. The hardships endured during his early years gave him an appreciation of the trials of the common people and solidified his desire to assist them.

Confucius' success as a great teacher and philosopher was built upon failures in the world of politics. He never was elected or selected to influential offices he sought early in his career, but later advised the top Chinese leaders of his day. Within a relatively short period following his death, Confucius was regarded throughout China as "the mentor and model of ten thousand generations."

Confucius wrote, "On reaching the age of fifteen, I bent my mind to learning." In his early twenties, having held several insignificant government posts, he established himself as a tutor, much along the lines of Socrates. His reputation spread quickly and he soon gained a band of disciples.

Like Socrates (469-399 B.C.) and Jesus, he engaged in dialogue and shared parables more than he lectured. As a result of his many dialogues and responses to questions, we have numerous "sayings" of Confucius today.

Confucius did not present himself as a saint or sage, but as a fellow traveler and searcher, endearing himself to his students and disciples. He emphasized that people must dispose of false "airs" and be totally real in order to establish the solid foundations needed for civilized society and for peace among all people.

According to Confucius:

If there is righteousness in the heart,
there will be beauty in character.
If there is beauty in character,
there will be harmony in the home.
If there is harmony in the home,
there will be order in the nation.
It there is order in the nation,
there will be peace in the world.

The overall goal of Confucianism is to educate people to be self-motivated, self-disciplined and able to assume personal responsibility. Reaching such a goal allows people to attain individual and group objectives, and leads to the attainment of an ideal, harmonious society.

Confucianism, when seen as an ethical and moral philosophy of life, has been merged with other philosophies and/or religions. For example, Chinese, Korean and Japanese bring together elements of Confucianism, Taoism and Buddhism. Confucianism is also a strong influence in other countries of Southeast Asia, as well as among people of Far Eastern descent living around the world.

CHRISTIANITY. The Jews have prophesied the coming of a Messiah and still await the coming. Christians believe that the prophecy was fulfilled in the birth of Jesus Christ.

The New Testament of the *Bible* records the life and teachings of Jesus of Nazareth, who was well versed in his religion of "the God of Abraham, the God of Isaac and the God of Jacob." Jesus emphasized the emerged Jewish belief that there is only one God.

At the same time, Jesus perceived that many of the Jews of his day had become caught up in a religion that consisted largely in external observances and rituals. He felt that too many of the Jewish leaders were ignoring the fact that God had called them to personal integrity and to be a blessing to others. He viewed the majority of the leaders as possessing very little spiritual humility; he emphasized a return to social righteousness and to a faith that produced good works.

There were other Jewish leaders of the day who shared the same perception, but they did not address the situation in such a confrontational way as Jesus did. One of the more notable of those who advocated that Judaism should "get back on track" was Rabbi Hillel, who was still living when Jesus was born. He preached love, universal fellowship and social concern, but found, as did Isaiah and others before him - and Jesus after him - too many people were content with the status quo.

Because Jesus was blunt and to the point, and because he preached that he was, indeed, the Messiah, Jesus' reception was a stormy one. People grew to either love him or hate him. There was no middle ground. He could not be ignored.

Eventually, Jesus was crucified on a cross and, according to Christian belief, was resurrected to eternal life. To Christians, the moment Jesus died he took upon his shoulders all the sins that had ever been committed, all the sins that were being committed and all that would ever be committed. Christians believe that if a person will ask for forgiveness and accept Jesus as the Messiah (the Christ), their sins will be forgiven and they will spend eternity with God the Father, the Son (Jesus) and the Holy Spirit.

Jesus emphasized that a person is "saved" through faith, not good works. However, he and New Testament writers also emphasized that if the faith is real, then the good works will come. It is like a circle: stepping out on faith and being "saved" by grace, resulting in the production of good works.

Jesus' teaching and preaching was passed along verbally until the earliest writings of the New Testament appeared between A.D. 50-75. The *Pauline Epistles* came into being during this time, followed by the *Acts of The Apostles*, written by Luke the physician. The four *Gospels* were recorded between approximately A.D. 65-150.

In these writings and in the other books of the New Testament, the virgin birth and the idea that Jesus is the Son of God is emphasized. His birth in the Bethlehem stable, his baptism by John the Baptist, his temptation by Satan, his ministry of preaching, teaching and healing in Galilee, and his momentous trip to Jerusalem are all covered. Jesus is presented as the great *Teacher*, who has the authority to interpret the Law of God.

Interestingly, some observers feel there are Christian practices today which contradict the faith affirmations and moral imperatives upon which the religion was founded. Just as Jesus accused the Jews of his day of departing from "the God of Abraham, the God of Isaac and the God of Jacob," accusations today point toward Christians departing from Christ.

Observers point out that while preaching from the Scriptures, Christian communities often find themselves consenting to racist, sexist, classist, naturist and ecclesiastical practices which Christ would not approve.

Whatever one's feelings on contemporary Christianity, with approximately 33 of every 100 inhabitants of our global community professing Christianity, a noticeable change would take place in our world overnight if at least one-half of the 33 would immediately adhere to all the Christian principles set forth in this book.

ISLAM. Even though many people view Islam as beginning with the birth of Muhammad in approximately A.D. 570, Muslims (followers of the Islam religion) claim that their religion was founded by God, "In the beginning," and that Muhammad is the last and greatest of many great prophets.

Muslims accept the Old Testament of the Bible and the teachings of Jesus in the New Testament. Their own holy book, the *Koran*, continues the Old and New Testaments, and presents itself as their culmination: "We made a covenant of old with the Children of Israel and you have nothing of guidance until you observe the Torah and the Gospel."

The Koran refers to God as *Allah*, an Arabic word formed by joining the article *"al"* (the) with *Ilah* (God). Literally, *Allah* means "the God." The Hebrew word for the plural majesty of God is *Elohim*. When the plural ending *"im"* is dropped, the two words sound much alike.

Like the Jews, Muslims see themselves as descendants of Abraham. In the Old Testament, it is recorded that Abraham married Sarah, and had no children. So Sarah took her maid, an Egyptian girl named Hagar (whom many Muslims believe was black and the second wife of Abraham rather than a concubine), and gave her to Abraham. He slept with her, and Hagar became pregnant. Sarah felt the girl grew arrogant, so she gained permission from Abraham to punish the girl.

Hagar ran away, but an angel stopped her and told her to return to Abraham and Sarah. The angel also told Hagar that she would have a son and that the boy should be named Ishmael ("God hears"), because God had heard Hagar's woes. She returned and Ishmael was born.

Later, Sarah became pregnant and gave birth to Isaac. To make sure that Isaac did not have to share Abraham's inheritance with Ishmael, Sarah asked Abraham to send Hagar and Ishmael away. Abraham protested, but God said that Isaac was the son through whom his promises to Abraham would be fulfilled. He told Abraham to send away Hagar and Ishmael, but that he would also make a nation of the descendants of Ishmael since he, too, was Abraham's son.

According to the Koran, Ishmael went to the place where Mecca was to rise. His descendants, flourishing in Arabia, became Muslims, while the descendants of Isaac, who remained in Palestine, became the nation of Israel.

Ishmael's lineage in Arabia, according to Islam, led to Muhammad, the prophet the Muslims consider to be the last authentic prophet of God.

Muhammad was born into a crude, ignorant world, but was born into the leading tribe of Mecca, the Koreish. His name means "highly praised." His father died a few days prior to his birth and his mother died when he was six. His grandfather began to raise him, but died when the boy was eight.

Muhammad was passed along to be reared by his uncle, a shepherd. Because of the way he responded to the hard work in caring for the flocks, he was warmly accepted into the family.

The early, difficult life he experienced led him to become highly sensitive to human suffering. As he grew into adulthood, his desire to help others also grew.

As a young man, Muhammad got into the caravan business, which led him to enter the service of a wealthy widow named Khadija. They married and were said to be a great match, even though he was 25 and she was 40. The marriage also allowed him time to prepare for a ministry that he would begin 15 years later.

For long periods of time, he would frequent a mountain on the outskirts of Mecca, known as Mount Hira. Here, in a cave, he would meditate and study. In that cave, Muhammad heard a voice tell him, "You are the appointed one." He also heard the command to, "Proclaim!"

Just as Moses, Jeremiah, Gideon and others of the Old Testament resisted a command to proclaim, so did Muhammad. But following the experience in the cave, he felt that from then on his life was not his own and was not under his control but under the leadership of Allah.

Even though much of the Islam doctrine parallels Judaism and Christianity, and actually builds upon them, there are major differences. For example, Islam honors Jesus as a prophet and accepts his virgin birth, but does not accept the Incarnation and Trinity as professed by Christians. Neither does Islam accept Jews as the singularly chosen people of God.

Conflicts exist between Islam and other Judeo-Christian concepts, but in getting back to the basics of the three religions, the idea of true faith leading to good works and peace among people is emphasized. This emphasis is also shared by the other three religions.

IN SUMMARY: The six religions have definite,

distinguishable differences. However, they also have much in common concerning *"the way a person should live."*

Buddhism was built upon Hinduism, and many of the principles and teachings of these two are found in the other four. Christianity was built upon Judaism, and Islam was built upon a combination of these two. Meanwhile, Confucianism appears to be an ethical and moral philosophy/religion of living that closely parallels the other five.

In totality, yes, each of the religions is quite different from the rest. As I emphasized earlier, however, when proponents of the religions adhere to the parallel principles, then relationships between people, within families and among nations can be strengthened.

- Carl Mays

Put Faith Into Action

A person who merely knows right principles is not equal to the person who loves them. A person who merely talks right principles is not equal to the person who does them.

Confucianism

Like a beautiful flower, full of color, but without scent, are the fine but fruitless words of one who does not act accordingly.

Buddhism

Students, teachers and others who read the mere words of ponderous books, know nothing. They only waste time in vain pursuit of words; the person who acts righteously is wise.

Hinduism

Put Faith Into Action

The chief thing is not in the learning, it is in the doing.

Judaism

Follow up words with actions; and follow up bad actions with good, so as to wipe them out; and behave in a decent way to people.

Islam

What good is it for you to say that you have faith if your actions do not prove it? Can that faith save you? Suppose there are brothers and sisters who need clothes and don't have enough to eat. What good is there in saying to them, "God bless you! Keep warm and eat well!" - if you don't give them the necessities of life? So it is with faith: if it is alone and includes no actions, then it is dead.

Christianity

Love Others

To the person in whom love dwells, the whole world is but one family.

Buddhism

Humans are like pillow-cases. The color of one may be red, that of another blue, that of a third black, but all contain the same cotton.

Hinduism

Love everyone. Know everyone.

Confucianism

Love Others

Don't take revenge on anyone. Don't bear
a grudge. Love your neighbor as yourself.

Judaism

Little children, let us stop just saying we love
people; let us really love them, and show it by
our actions.

Christianity

No one of you is a true believer until you love
for your brother and sister what you love for
yourself.

Islam

Work For Peace

Blessed are those who work for peace; God will call them his children!

Christianity

How wonderful it is to see a messenger coming across the mountains bringing good news, the news of peace!

Judaism

Shall I tell you what acts are better than fasting, charity and prayers? Making peace between enemies are such acts; for enmity and malice tear up the heavenly rewards by the roots.

Islam

Work For Peace

The wise person cultivates a friendly harmony, without being weak.

Confucianism

When righteousness is practiced to win peace, one who so walks shall gain the victory and all fetters utterly destroy.

Buddhism

The noble minded dedicate themselves to the promotion of peace and the happiness of others - even those who injure them.

Hinduism

Live In Unity

Behold, how good and pleasant it is when
people dwell in unity!

Judaism

In dealing with people, practice five things:
generosity, sincerity, earnestness, kindness and
seriousness.

Confucianism

When you have love in your heart, all people
are brothers and sisters. It is only the narrow-
minded that make such distinctions as, "This is
our friend; that is our enemy."

Buddhism

Live In Unity

God has made of one blood all the nations and all the races of people.

Christianity

With God as the head, humans are as parts of the body unto one another, having one common womb, mind and spirit.

Hinduism

All creatures are the family of God; and he is the most beloved of God who does good unto his family.

Islam

Live Your Professed Beliefs

Common people talk bagfuls of religion but act not a grain of it, while the wise person speaks little, but whose whole life is a religion acted out.

Hinduism

Are there still some among you who think that "believing" is all you have to do? When will you ever learn that "believing" amounts to nothing until you do what God wants you to do?

Christianity

Constantly read the book of the Law in worship. Study it diligently and make sure you obey everything written in it. Then you will succeed . . . How can one live a pure life? By reading God's Word and following its rules.

Judaism

Live Your Professed Beliefs

A person who knows the precepts by heart, but fails to practice them, is like someone who lights a lamp and then shuts both *eyes*.

Buddhism

To see what is right and not do it, is lack of courage.

Confucianism

There is no piety in turning your faces towards the east or the west, but one is pious who believes in God . . . who for the love of God disburses personal wealth; observes prayer and pays legal alms; is faithful to engagements; and is patient under ills and hardships in time of trouble.

Islam

Apply The Scriptures

Study the words, no doubt, but look behind them to the thought they indicate. And having found it, throw the words away as chaff when you have sifted out the grain.

Hinduism

It is best to let a letter be uprooted than to allow the meaning of the Torah to be forgotten.

Judaism

The Koran was sent down in seven dialects, and in every one of its sentences there is an outer and an inner meaning to discern.

Islam

Apply The Scriptures

All Scripture is inspired by God and is useful to teach us what is true and to help us to realize what is wrong. It corrects us and helps us to do the right thing. It equips us and prepares us to do good.

Christianity

The strength of kindness is my abode; the apparel of self-control is my robe; and mental purity is my seat; let the preacher with all his words take his stand on this and preach.

Buddhism

It is not wise to let the words obstruct the deeds.

Confucianism

Accept
Personal Responsibility

The root of the empire is the state. The root of the state is the family. The root of the family is the person of its head.

Confucianism

As the person acts, so the person is. One becomes pure by good deeds and soiled by bad deeds. The deeds determine the person; and the deeds determine the rewards.

Hinduism

One does not become blessed because of plaited hair, mode of dress, family or birth; the person is blessed in whom there is truth and righteousness.

Buddhism

Accept Personal Responsibility

With one's own sins, a wicked person sets his or her own trap. Because of the absence of self-control and the presence of stupidity, the person is led away into darkness.

Judaism

For in its own works lies the fate of every soul.

Islam

A good person produces good deeds from a good heart. A bad person produces bad deeds from a bad heart. From the mouth overflows that of which the heart is full.

Christianity

Know Yourself

First take the log out of your own eye, and then you will see clearly to remove the speck from the eye of another.

Christianity

One is wise who knows others; one is far wiser who knows self.

Islam

Don't get into needless fights, nor grumble and complain about others. Are you yourself above criticism? If you are willing to be corrected, you are on the pathway to life.

Judaism

Know Yourself

If your love is not returned, if your leadership is rejected, if your politeness is met with rudeness, if your life is unfulfilled, then turn inward and examine yourself.

Confucianism

The faults of others we see easily; our own faults are very difficult to see. One's own self conquered is better than all other people.

Buddhism

With the beginning of self-discovery comes the beginning of wisdom. With wisdom, you ask to be forgiven if you have sinned against one who loves you, have wronged a brother or sister, have trespassed against a neighbor or stranger.

Hinduism

Do Not Judge Others

The good show pity even to seemingly worthless beings, not judging them. The moon does not withhold its light from the hovel of the outcast.

Hinduism

Do not judge your neighbor until you are in your neighbor's place.

Judaism

Follow that which is revealed to you, and persevere with patience until God shall judge; for he is the best judge.

Islam

Do Not Judge Others

Judge not, and you shall not be judged;
condemn not, and you shall not be
condemned.

Christianity

Do not judge others. Be tolerant with the
intolerant, mild with the violent and free from
greed among the greedy.

Buddhism

If you want to nourish a bird, you should let it
live the way it chooses. Creatures differ because
they have different likes and dislikes. Therefore,
sages never require the same ability from all
creatures.

Confucianism

Be Considerate Of Others

Do unto others as you would have them do unto you, for this is the law and the prophets.

Christianity

That which one desires not for oneself, do not do unto others.

Buddhism

Treat others as you would want to be treated. Do nothing to your neighbor which you would not have your neighbor do to you.

Hinduism

Be Considerate Of Others

What is hurtful to yourself do not to others.
That is the whole of the Torah and the
remainder is but commentary.

Judaism

Do unto others as you would wish to have done
unto you; and reject for others what you would
reject for yourselves.

Islam

What you do not want done to yourself, do not
do to others.

Confucianism

Forgive Others

Forgive, if you wish to be forgiven.

Hinduism

Only a forgiving spirit can free us to be forgiven.

Buddhism

Forgive not only with your mouth, but also with your heart.

Confucianism

Forgive Others

Stop being mean, bad-tempered and angry. Quarreling, harsh words and dislike of others should have no place in your lives. Instead, be kind to each other, tenderhearted, forgiving one another, just as God has forgiven you.

Christianity

The most beautiful thing one person can do for another is to forgive wrong.

Judaism

Be prepared to forgive others seventy times a day.

Islam

Heed Your Conscience

Righteousness is what the soul and the heart feel tranquil about; and sinfulness is what is fixed in the soul, and roams about in the breast, even if people give their decisions in your favor over and over again.

Islam

The person who knows right from wrong, and has the good judgement and common sense to apply it in thought, speech and actions, is much happier than a person who is merely rich with material possessions!

Judaism

Let us abstain from stealing; from adultery; from lying; from evil speaking; from abuse; from idle talk; from covetousness; from ill-will; from false opinions. Let us now abstain from all these things we know are wrong.

Buddhism

Heed Your Conscience

You will find happiness and will not sin if you do what you truly believe is right. But if you believe that something is wrong and do it anyway, you will sin and find unhappiness. If you believe it is right, for you it is right; if you believe it is wrong, for you it is wrong.

Christianity

Do not do what your own sense of righteousness tells you not to do, and do not desire what your sense of righteousness tells you not to desire; to act thus is all you have to do.

Confucianism

Let the scriptures be your authority, in determining what ought to be done, or what ought not to be done. Knowing what has been declared by the ordinances of the scriptures, one ought to live in this world.

Hinduism

Be Truthful

One who is truly enlightened is incapable of deliberately telling lies.

Buddhism

Sit in the assembly of the honest; join with those that are good and virtuous; have nothing to do with the unrighteous.

Hinduism

Stop lying to each other; tell the truth, for we are parts of each other and when we lie to each other we are hurting ourselves.

Christianity

Be Truthful

Speak truth to your neighbor; execute the judgement of truth and peace in your gates.

Judaism

Sincerity and truth are the basis of every virtue.

Confucianism

Do not clothe the truth with falsehood; do not knowingly conceal the truth.

Islam

Be Generous To Others

The poor, the orphan, the captive - feed them
for the love of God alone, desiring no reward,
nor even thanks.

Islam

God blesses those who are kind to the poor;
the Lord will help them when they are in
trouble.

Judaism

It is more blessed to give than to receive.

Christianity

Be Generous To Others

The greatest wealth consists in being charitable, and the greatest happiness in having tranquility of mind.

Buddhism

Wisdom, benevolence, and fortitude, these are the universal virtues.

Confucianism

Bounteous is the person who gives to the feeble beggar who comes in want of food.

Hinduism

Do Worthy Deeds

I say unto you: deeds of love are worth as much as all the commandments of the law.

Judaism

God will give each person whatever the person's deeds deserve..

Christianity

One should say, "I am not concerned that I am not known; I seek to be worthy to be known by the deeds I do."

Confucianism

Do Worthy Deeds

If you derive pleasure from the good which you do, and are grieved by the evil which you commit, then you are a true believer.

Islam

Success is born of action and deeds. Whatsoever a great person does, others also do; the standard this person sets up, by that the people go.

Hinduism

Let the motive be in the deed. If the motive is right, the deed's results are multiplied and happiness is increased.

Buddhism

Cherish Friends

My commandment is this: love one another, just as I love you. The greatest love one can have for friends is to sacrifice one's life for them.

Christianity

Do not forsake each other; do not lie to each other; do not oppress each other.

Islam

Friendship should be maintained without any presumption on the ground of one's age, or station, or the circumstances of relatives. Friendship with a person is friendship with the person's virtue, and does not admit of assumptions of superiority.

Confucianism

Cherish Friends

A true friend is always loyal, and a brother or sister is always ready to help in times of trouble.

Judaism

There is none more happy than the person who has a friend to converse with and to share life with.

Hinduism

Be humble and meek if you would be exalted. Praise everyone's good qualities if you would have friends.

Buddhism

Choose Associates Carefully

Keep away from people who are angry and short-tempered; you may become like them and endanger your very souls.

Judaism

If you adjust your weights to those of the untrue, you will fall into deficiency and falseness, and your intellect will become confused.

Islam

Sit in the assembly of the honest; combine with those that are good and virtuous; and have nothing to do with the wicked and the unrighteous.

Hinduism

Choose Associates Carefully

Feel kindly toward everyone, but be intimate only with the virtuous.

Confucianism

Stay apart from those who see sin where there is no sin, and see no sin where there is sin. Embracing false doctrines, they enter the evil path.

Buddhism

Have the discipline to keep away from things that give you evil thoughts, but stay close to anything that causes you to want to do what is right. Have faith and love, and enjoy the companionship of those who love the Lord and have pure hearts.

Christianity

Do Not Be Envious

If you love your neighbor as much as you love yourself, you will not want to harm, cheat, kill or steal from your neighbor. And you won't sin with your neighbor's spouse or want anything that your neighbor has, or do anything else the Ten Commandments say is wrong.

Christianity

One who is enlightened is not covetous with desires, not fierce with longings, not malevolent of heart, not of mind corrupt. In seeking personal happiness, one who punishes or kills beings who also long for happiness, will not find happiness after death.

Buddhism

One who acts with a constant view to personal gain or advantage while disregarding the rights and souls of others will be much murmured against.

Confucianism

Do Not Be Envious

Do not envy another person's house. Do not desire to sleep with another's wife or husband. Do not want another's workers, cattle, donkeys or anything else the person has.

Judaism

From covetousness anger proceeds; from covetousness lust is born; from covetousness come delusion and perdition. Covetousness is the cause of sin. He who looks on another's wife as a mother, on another's goods as a clod of earth, and on all creatures as himself, is a wise person.

Hinduism

Do not be envious of each other; and do not hate each other. Do not oppose each other. Place your efforts in building up rather than tearing down. A person's life, property and honor are not to be violated by another person.

Islam

Seek Wisdom

Happy is the person that finds wisdom and gets understanding. How much better it is to get wisdom than gold, and to get understanding rather than silver!

Judaism

To be fond of learning is to be near to knowledge. Ignorance is the night of the mind, but a night without moon or star.

Confucianism

Knowledge is the best treasure that one can obtain. Learning is the revered of the revered. It is learning that enables a person to better the condition of friends and relations. Knowledge and love of God are ultimately one and the same. There is no difference between pure knowledge and pure love.

Hinduism

Seek Wisdom

If you have wisdom, it will be shown to others by your good deeds, humility and understanding. Wisdom from God is pure and full of quiet gentleness. It is peace-loving and courteous. It allows discussion and is willing to listen to others. Those who have wisdom will plant seeds of peace and reap a harvest of goodness.

Christianity

One who pursues true wisdom brightens up this world like the moon set free from the clouds. The real treasure is that laid up through charity and piety, temperance and self-control.

Buddhism

Seek knowledge from the cradle to the grave. Riches are not from an abundance of worldly goods, but from a contented mind.

Islam

Control Your Anger

One who holds back rising anger like a rolling chariot is a real driver; other people are but holding the reins.

Buddhism

When anger rises, think of the consequences.

Confucianism

Everyone should be quick to listen, slow to speak and slow to become angry, for one's anger does not bring about the righteous life that God desires. Do not let the sun go down while you are still angry.

Christianity

Control Your Anger

A gentle answer quiets anger; harsh words lead to quarrels. Quick tempers cause arguments; patience brings peace. If you are wise, you will control your temper. A person without self-control is as defenseless as a city with broken-down walls.

Judaism

A man said to the prophet, "Give me a command." The prophet replied, "Do not get angry." The man repeated the question several times, and the prophet said, "Do not get angry."

Islam

He who gives up anger attains to God.

Hinduism

Overcome Wrong With Right

Overcome anger by love; overcome evil by good; overcome the greedy by generosity; overcome the liar by truth.

Buddhism

Love your enemies and pray for those who persecute you.

Christianity

Recompense evil; conquer it with good.

Islam

Overcome
Wrong With Right

If your enemy is hungry, feed him; if he is thirsty, give him a drink. This will make him feel ashamed of himself, and God will reward you.

Judaism

With kindness conquer rage; with goodness conquer malice; with generosity defeat all meanness; with the straight truth defeat lies and deceit.

Hinduism

Recompense injury with justice, and unkindness with kindness.

Confucianism

Choose Words Carefully

Kind words bear pleasant fruit; careless words destroy the spirit and lead to trouble.

Judaism

The wise person is one who is slow in choosing words and earnest in conduct.

Confucianism

Double-tongued are the snakes and the malicious; their cruel mouths are the source of many an evil.

Hinduism

Choose Words Carefully

Do not speak harshly to anyone; those who are spoken to will answer you in the same way.

Buddhism

If you can control your tongue, it proves you have perfect control over yourself in every other way. The tongue is a small thing, but it can do great damage.

Christianity

Although your words appear uniform and in harmony, they are the source, in their effect, of contention and anger.

Islam

Plant Wisely

A generous person will be enriched, and one who waters will be watered.

Judaism

Whatever a person sows, that also will the person reap.

Christianity

One cannot gather what one does not sow; as one does plant the tree, so it will grow.

Hinduism

Plant wisely

It is nature's rule, that as we sow, we shall reap.

Buddhism

Actions are to be judged only in accordance with intentions; and one gets only what one intended.

Islam

What proceeds from you will return to you. Constant activity in doing good, and endeavoring to make others happy, is one of the surest ways of making ourselves so.

Confucianism

Be Diligent

The expectations of life depend upon diligence; if you wish to perfect your work, you must first sharpen your tools. In all things, success depends upon previous preparation, and without it there is sure to be failure.

Confucianism

A person unwilling to work soon experiences failure, but the diligent worker will attain success.

Judaism

If anything is to be done, let a person do it vigorously! Better it would be to swallow a heated iron ball, like flaring fire, than that a bad, unrestrained person should live on the charity of the land.

Buddhism

Be Diligent

Whoever refuses to work is not allowed to eat. We command these people and warn them to lead orderly lives and work to earn their own living.

Christianity

Six faults ought to be avoided by one seeking success: too much sleep, sloth, laziness, fear, anger and too much talk.

Hinduism

When bodily needs are met, higher concerns can flower.

Islam

Use Money Wisely

Let the rich satisfy the poor implorer, and bend their eyes upon a longer pathway. Riches come now to one, now to another, and like the wheels are ever rolling.

Hinduism

Don't horde treasures here on earth where they can be destroyed or stolen. Invest them in heaven where their value is secure and thieves can never steal them. Where your treasures are, that is where your heart will be.

Christianity

There are people dying from famine, and you do not know to issue the stores of your granaries for them. When people die, you say, "It is not owing to me; it is owing to the year." How does this differ from stabbing and killing a person, and then saying, "It was not I, it was the weapon"?

Confucianism

Use Money Wisely

One who is truly enlightened is incapable of laying up treasure for indulgence in worldly pleasure.

Buddhism

Consume not your wealth among yourselves in vain things; nor offer it to judges as a bribe that you may consume a part of others' wealth unjustly, while you know the sin which you commit.

Islam

Lord, may I not live my life merely gaining riches that someone else will spend. May I find my contentment and hope in knowing you.

Judaism

Practice True Humility

Humility is the solid foundation of all the virtues.

Confucianism

One who eagerly takes credit when something is successful, and eagerly throws the blame when something goes wrong, and who always looks for faults in the wise and righteous - this person is without humility and possesses the nature of a crow.

Buddhism

Put on the apron of humility to serve one another, for God blesses those who are humble but resists those who are puffed up with pride.

Christianity

Practice True Humility

Arrogance and haughtiness will lead to destruction; true humility will lead to honors.

Judaism

One who remains humble, requiring much from self and little from others, will keep from being the object of resentment.

Confucianism

God is a sufficient witness between you and me: He knows all that is in the heavens and the earth, and they who are vain, believing in vain things and disbelieving in God - these shall suffer loss.

Islam

Honor Your Parents

Honor your father and your mother, so that you may live a long time in the land that the Lord your God gives you.

Judaism

To support Father and Mother,
To cherish Spouse and Child,
To follow a peaceful calling,
This is the greatest blessing.

Buddhism

Children, obey your parents in the Lord; for this is the right thing to do.

Christianity

Honor Your Parents

Serve and revere your parents. Heaven is spread beneath the feet of mothers everywhere.

Islam

If each of you would love your parents and show due respect to your elders, the whole empire would enjoy tranquility.

Confucianism

Honor your Father and Mother. Forget not the favors you have received.

Hinduism

Respect The Elderly

To honor an elderly person is to show respect for God.

Islam

Learn from the elderly sages. A person who is full of faith obtains wisdom and has mastery over the senses. The fixtures and furniture of one's house may be stolen by thieves; but knowledge is above stealing.

Hinduism

Treat with reverence the elders in your own family.

Confucianism

Respect The Elderly

Four things will increase for the person who always greets and constantly reveres the aged: life, beauty, power, happiness.

Buddhism

The elderly have obtained wisdom and with their years they have gained understanding.

Judaism

Do not rebuke an elder, but treat this person as you would treat a loving father or mother.

Christianity

Have Child-Like Faith

Great people have the nature of children. They are always children before God, so they have no egoism. Their strength is of God, belonging to him and coming from him, nothing of themselves. If one does not have simple, child-like faith, one does not get divine illumination.

Hinduism

The great person is the one who does not lose his or her child's-heart.

Confucianism

Unless you become like children, you will never enter the Kingdom of heaven. The greatest among you is the one who is humble and has the faith of a child.

Christianity

Have Child-Like Faith

The wolf and the lamb will lie down side by side, and the leopard will be at peace with the goats. Calves and cattle will be safe among lions, and a little child will lead them all.

Judaism

If a person speaks or acts with pure thought, as a little child, happiness follows like a shadow that never leaves.

Buddhism

A deep child-like faith, a close attention to one's virtues and a love for brothers and sisters, these are the traits of a righteous and noble soul.

Islam

Find Strength Within

Some deluded people speak of nature, and others speak of time as the cause of everything; but it is the greatness of God by which this wheel is made to turn. He is the one God, dwelling in all. Strength and eternal happiness belong to the wise who perceive him within.

Hinduism

Seek the permanent, stable, imperishable, immovable power that is bliss and happiness. Seek the secure refuge, the shelter and the place of unassailable safety.

Buddhism

How vast is God, the ruler of us below! To the wise person he gives benevolence, righteousness, propriety and knowledge. These are rooted in the heart; their growth and manifestation are a mild harmony appearing in the countenance, a rich fullness in the back, and the character imparted to the four limbs.

Confucianism

Find Strength Within

God is our refuge and strength, a constant help in times of trouble. Therefore we will not fear, though the earth be removed, and though the mountains be carried into the midst of the sea.

Judaism

Give God the glory, for his mighty power at work within us is able to do much more than we would ever dare ask or even dream of - infinitely beyond our highest prayers, desires, thoughts or hopes. And, he provides us with a peace that is beyond all human understanding.

Christianity

God has been kind to us, and from the pestilential torment of the scorching wind he has preserved us. We called upon him, the Beneficent, the Merciful.

Islam

Pray

Praise be to God, the Lord of all creatures . . .
Direct us in the right way, in the way of those to
whom you have been gracious . . .

Islam

Our prayer is that every living creature will
abound in well-being and peace; that every
living creature - weak or strong, big or small,
far or near, seen or unseen, already born or
awaiting birth - may attain peace.

Buddhism

When you go to your knees in true and deep
humility as a servant, only then can you rise to
lead.

Confucianism

Pray

The true, earnest prayer of a righteous person has great power and can accomplish wonderful results.

Christianity

I will call upon the Lord to save me, and he will. I will pray morning, noon and night; and he will hear and answer.

Judaism

Supreme Lord, guide us by the right path to happiness, and give us strength and will to war against the sins that rage in us and lead us astray. We bow in reverence and prayer to you, Lord.

Hinduism

About The Author

Carl Mays, CSP, CPAE, is a speaker and consultant in the areas of leadership and human relations. He has spoken to over 2500 groups, including corporations, associations, religious institutions, sports teams, schools and universities. He is a member of the National Speakers Association's *Speaker Hall of Fame*.

Carl served as president of Religious Heritage of America, an organization that promotes the high ideals and values upon which America was founded. RHA chairman W. Clement Stone presented him with the *National Faith & Freedom Award* for his contributions as a communicator.

Carl earned an undergraduate degree in oral and written communications and a graduate degree in religious education. He has taught an adult Bible class for 24 years and has worked with young people through the Fellowship of Christian Athletes for 21 years. He has counseled at a home for unwed mothers, an international marine hospital and a charity hospital. His presentation, *World Religions - Distilled*, is well received by both secular and religious groups.

Other books by Carl include *A Strategy For Winning, Winning Thoughts, Anatomy Of A Leader and Prayers From The Heart*. He and his wife, Jean, live in Gatlinburg, Tennessee.

You may visit **www.carlmays.com** for additional insight into Carl's work.